Heart Full of Spleen:

Selected Poems and Lyrics

2003 - 2007

Published by
Giant Self Publishing
622 W. Greenville Rd.
Scituate, RI 02857

If you purchased this book without a cover,
good for you.

ISBN: 978-0-6151-7833-2

First Edition
November, 2007

To Suzi,

For Everything,

Of Course.

A Note To The Reader:

Dear Reader,

   Thank you for making it this far. If you finish this sentence, and close the book, set it down, and never look at it again, no one will ever know. If you choose to continue, please feel free to read the pieces that follow in any order, as much or as little as you like.
   This volume represents a collection of scraps. A shoebox full of receipts, or a junk drawer crammed with the detritus of forgotten instants. Much of what follows are lyrics for songs, written over the last half-decade. Many were conceived or intended for bands which broke apart or never fully formed. Some have never been sung at all.
   It comes as a surprise to many when they learn that their created works possess an identity, and a power, all their own. Songs, paintings, pictures, poems, all grow into a Golem-like strength and vitality independent of artistic intention. Many simply refuse to remain alone with the person or people responsible for their creation. This vitality, along with the spooky, supersensible intelligence that many works of art possess, conspires to tell us more about our lives and our selves than we truly wish to know.
   Like the invisible players of forgotten times, the genius loci and daemon lords, our creative endeavors magnify our smallest, cruelest, most short-sighted desires by showing us exactly what we claim to want. In many ancient cultures, the shadowy occupants of mostly invisible realms are directly responsible for the gifts of song, painting, language, and prayer. Gifts from these entities are universally ambivalent, mired in the duality of

creatures fed on dark underground energies.

Songs hate to go unsung. However we choose to express our deepest truths, hidden in plain sight in the corners of our junk drawers, those expressions demand the light of day. Or perhaps they would prefer, like the Surem and the Shedim of old, to be glimpsed only at night.

The pieces that follow were mine for awhile. I tended to them as carefully as I knew how, with a great deal of sincere love and effort. They belong now to anyone who continues on to read them.

And with that, you've been warned. Remember what I said about putting the book down now. No one will ever know. If you choose to continue, I hope you find something to enjoy somewhere inside these pages. Whether you love or hate any or all of these scraps, they belong to you now. Treat them well, or I'm coming to get you, like in a Waylon Jennings' song.

Thank You,
Thaddeus Denton
November 15, 2007

"Those who live, live off the dead."

-Antonin Artaud

-

God knows where you've gone
and now the sunlight makes me nervous.
I'm staying up 'til dawn.
I'm in your late-night Secret Service.

-

<u>the pillars of creation</u>

everybody's gonna be
forever young and pretty
everybody's gonna walk
the streets of New York City
one day we'll all be deified
in coffee table books
and future generations
will adore the way we look

and there's sex to have in bathrooms
and there's drugs to do in cars
there's the pillars of creation
for all us hot, young stars

get yourself a label
so the people know your name
pull up to the table
and we'll deal you in the game
it's not the cards you're holding
it's the way you make 'em lie
when you take it in the mouth
be sure you look 'em in the eye

and there's friends to leave behind you
someone brand new to become

there's the pillars of creation
in the paper on your tongue

sickened and exhausted,
head full of the past
add a dash of bitter to
the damage in your glass
try to get it down
before it tumbles from your hand
hope it shatters hard enough
to turn back into sand

and there's someone there to sweep it up
and get it in the trash
there's the pillars of creation
but they're only dust and ash

self-titled

there are chains of tears that bind us
like a needless surgery
there are haunted years behind us
and the future's plain to see
we have starved in times of plenty
like a city in the sea
i'm the rust across your chrome
and you're the thumbprint on my penny

we have shared in subtle powers
like a painted misery
we've put fire to the flowers
meant to set some orphan free
we have built a mighty tower
to inevitability
i'm the rust across your chrome
you're the thumbprint on my penny

there are spaces carved in silence
like a family history
there's a caul we cut from kindness
and a cloak of cruelty
there's a breeze that's singing sweetly
through an ancient gallows tree
i'm the rust across your chrome

and you're the thumbprint on my penny

there's the sorrow of the dust
and there's the tragedy of leaves
there's a mother grown too deaf
to hear her child's desperate pleas
and between it all your smile
comes with style, comes with ease

i'm the rust across your chrome
and you're the thumbprint on my penny

it doesn't matter now

it doesn't matter now
about what could have been instead
the things that you accomplished
in the life you might have led
and all that you deserve
that life never quite allowed
i'm sure it's all my fault
but it doesn't matter now

it doesn't matter now
what was promised from the cross
the words they may endure
but the meaning's all been lost
it's all been torn to pieces
like the earth beneath the plow
it used to make us whole
but it doesn't matter now

it doesn't matter now
about the man i used to be
the words i tried to write
that they might match your melody
i know i did it one time
but i can't remember how
and as far as i can tell

it doesn't matter now

it doesn't matter now
about the Garden and the Tree
it's true, i dropped a dime on you
but first you lied to me
and all that followed cast
a different light upon the Vow
it used to make me crazy
but it doesn't matter now

ailment (a lament)

in this corridor of worship
with a prayer upon each fingertip
in darkness, like some ancient, blinded seer
i traced each line of muscle
like the surgeon with his scalpel
neither one of us enough to keep you here

<u>i got you</u>

what foretells an occupation
incubates abomination
horror wears a doll's complexion
painted bright with kind intention

but i got you,
for a minute or two
ash-blue in a cigarette room
trussed-up brand new
like a shotgun groom
yeah, i got you.
yeah, i got you.

dictate pace and prolong lives
like action stories serialized
the captain dies, the whale survives
the ships circle the sacrifice

but i got you,
like a souvenir tune
lunatic blue
in a paper-white room
drunk at noon
singing songs of the tomb
oh, i got you.

yes, i got you.

i got you
and you'll always be true
option-less blue
in a windowless room
stomach-less gut
like a portent of doom
but, i got you.
yeah, i got you.

-

you're the personal third-person
you're the instant archetype
hand-to-mouth
lift up your tongue
I know just where you hide

-

the party line

there's one in every kitchen
but the sounds are all the same
there's weeping in the Mission
muffled by the falling rain
for your sons have moved to cities
and they've left this land behind
but you can still destroy them
if you hold the party line

it's just to set a time
to find a better place to talk
it's just a flashing sign
to tell you when and where to walk
a realcoolworld is waiting
waiting for you to define
you never know who's listening
to the same old party line

grind your teeth and hold it
tell yourself you can control it
when you close your eyes you own it
it's a fixture in your mind

blame the ones who must invent it
you've done nothing to prevent it

but you're welcome to resent it
it's the good old party line

from one there must come many
leave it over for the few
get your picture on the penny
the whole world is brave and new
well, you've leveraged all your lovers
keep on moving down that line
in the distance all that wailing
sounds just like the party line

well, you'll never have to worry
you can shove it from your mind
and you'll never have to hurry
'cause there's nothing left to find
if your vision's getting blurry
that don't mean you're going blind
we'll teach you what to tell yourself
about the party line

- - - - -

Pictures are better than people.
It's one thing I know to be true.
They stay where you put them.
And how you remember.
And they never grow tired of you.

Pictures are better than people.
Ask again and I'll tell you the same.
They fade with the seasons.
And crumble to pieces.
And never need someone to blame.

- - - - -

Kentucky Highway

Kentucky Highway,
Take me
Where I'd so much rather be
Take me to the neon lights
of Nashville, Tennessee
Stay my heart with honky-tonk,
Comfort me with whiskey
Cold, Kentucky Highway
Keep a lane open for me

Kentucky Highway,
Take me
Any way you want to run
In pourin' midnight rain
Or in the burnin' mornin' sun
Take me where nobody sees
The man that I've become
Old, Kentucky Highway
Don't remind me what I done

Kentucky Highway
Take me
Any which way that you go
Run me up to Illinois
Or down to Tupelo

Somewhere I'm a stranger
Where there's not a soul I know
Long, Kentucky Highway
Keep them headlights burnin' low

Kentucky Highway,
Save me
From the ones who keep me here
Save me from another night
Of fightin' back the tears
Save me from the loneliness
Save me from the fear
Black, Kentucky Highway
Take me far from all things near.

just a little something

well, watch these people closely
watch their eyes and watch their hands
and listen to their voices
when they're making their demands
the words aren't as important
as the throbbing of their glands

'cause the devil's in the lord,
the devil's in the lord,
the devil's in the lord of this world.

see this shadow stretched before you
well, he never was a man
and the language that he's speaking
you don't want to understand
well, it's just a little something
for the trembling in your hands

but the devil's in the lord,
the devil's in the lord,
the devil's in the lord of this world.

well, they go astray from day one
speaking lies into the night
strangers to the womb that

spit them screaming into life
but it's not so much they're asking
just a piece of space and light

and the devil's in the lord,
the devil's in the lord,
the devil's in the lord of this world.

well, remember why you came here
what you hoped to take away
but the hours can last months here
while the years tick past like days
somewhere, someone misses you
someday you'll make her pay

because the devil's in the lord,
the devil's in the lord
the devil's in the lord of your world.

restaurant bathrooms

the farther you walk, the harder you're fucked
and my boots are split and dripping blood
red-line eyes burn mongrelized,
blink sand and teardrop mud

some old, glass cunt, inept at what
just stands there with her ears plugged shut
in sodden rags sick bodies dance,
feet scraping out a rut

i'm walking green around the lines
etched out under your eyes
restaurant bathrooms painted red
florescent blemished white

so drop your rig, grin big yellow
it's only shit when you have to swallow
your mouth is full tonight,
but you won't taste it by tomorrow

i'm walking green around the lines
cut up under your nose
restaurant bathrooms painted shut
a brilliant, blood-stained rose

i'm walking green around the lines
etched out under your eyes
restaurant bathrooms painted red
florescent blemished white

- - - - -
I just can't recall
having loved you at all,
though I know
that, once, it was true.

I see you there now,
and I ask myself how
I ever looked fondly
on you.

You're such a stupid, little girl.

A stupid, little girl,
sitting with your legs crossed on the floor.

Stupid, little girl,
you're a stupid, little girl.

I can't believe I didn't see before.
- - - - -

-

all the signs horizons show
don't answer any questions

crooked teeth,
the picture's straight
the genes remain indentured

-

the answering service

minutes like servants
of paranoid time
stay in a room
but it's different each night
no ones like sales ones
to draw me outside

the answering service is ruining my life.

stricken on linen
no cotton supply
climbing the walls
but it can't get you high
someone must be here
i don't look quite right

the answering service is bleeding me dry

the flowers that last night forgot
are the brilliant black pills on the countertop

but they don't make anything stop
it all just rings and rings and rings....

hours like dollars

are passing you by
the guy on the corner's
not there to supply
tie his shoe for him
he'll give you a dime

the answering service is ruining my life.

- - - - -
she does a great impression
of a terrible liar
she can start an argument
like a scout can start a fire
she'll take apart your day
and find a lifetime of suspense
she'll tell you things
that make your ears
curl up in self-defense

but no matter
rhyme nor reason
nor the season
nor the song

she does no wrong

she'll throw your broken body
from the balcony to the throng

she does no wrong
- - - - -

Judged and Found Wanting

I saw a little girl today
she looked just like you
you know the way my mind moves
once it moved in you too
I couldn't help but recall
all we put each other through
I've been judged and found wanting
and you know it's true

I saw an old man yesterday
I've tried hard not to see
he was what you might have been
that will now never be
while I sit here and weep
over your memory
I've been judged and found wanting
are you laughing at me?

I saw the same car as yours
with someone else at the wheel
and it's hard to describe
how it all made me feel
it was much like the rush
from the first time you steal
I've been judged and found wanting

and it does not seem real

I've been judged and found wanting
over and again
I've been judged and found wanting
in the eyes of all men
I've been judged and found wanting
for the crimes in my name
I've been judged and found wanting
yet still I remain

I saw your face in the crowd
but you never saw mine
they were braiding your hair
you were standing in line
you were asking them how
I could be so unkind
I've been judged and found wanting
for the very last time

I saw a cold sun go down
and I thought of you
all the the things I'll never say
everything you'll never do
and my lips on your skin
as it quickly turns blue
I've been judged and found wanting

and I'm coming back to you

I've been judged and found wanting
and I'm coming home to you

- - - - -

When I was just a child,
one especially weak and small,
one grey and lonely morning,
as the crimson leaves did fall,
I came upon a clearing,
and a man so thin and tall,
and we struck a bloody bargain,
to the distant church bell's call.

I sacrificed my youthhead
for The Story of Us All.

- - - - -

<u>running out of night</u>

the windows are behind us
that's the best that we can do
the goddamned sun reminds us
of the things we meant to do
the bed's still waiting for us,
but the room's gotten so bright
and it used to seem like something,
when we ran out of the night

now the bottles all are empty
and the lines have all been done
the phone's still here to tempt me
if the money weren't all gone
but my eyes are red as stopsigns,
and my skin feels far too tight
and we used to think we'd made it,
when we ran out of the night

there are places you could go to
just a few hours from now
there are people there who know you
who might comfort you, somehow
but the whole world's cheap and dirty,
in the rising morning light
and it used to feel like victory,

when we ran out of the night

maybe we were younger
and perhaps we were more kind
that brilliant, blinding hunger
isn't all we left behind
our blood's turned thin and angry,
and our bones aren't even white
and now it feels so lonely,
when we run out of the night

- - - - -
the streets are cracked
and broken
and i wish they'd finally sink
the lives you'll find are frozen
so let's have another
drink
at the bottom of this valley
we've all settled
far below
like a goddamned
dead-end alley
i'd go backwards
just to go

the streets are cracked and broken
hope you fall
and don't get up
the lives you'll find are frozen
so let's lift
another cup
at the bottom of this summer
everything
is thick with
sweat
like a goddamned dead-end lover
you just haven't

left her yet

- - - - -

-

I'm followin' the dollars
If you mind it, tell me so

Alot you got to holler,
Money makes the good times roll

-

He Will Not Come Again

man of shadows, man of sorrows
hanging sun in treetops bright
haggard mask of wool and copper
carved and scarred by blinding light

man of dust and man of toil
wind that tears the flesh from bone
man of sky and man of soil
silhouette of jagged stone

he is the desert of secret chambers
he is the scream from the filth of the manger
he is the face of the nationless stranger
he will not come again

man of peace and man of terror
gaunt as any starving child
man of death and man of rapture
name of everlasting trials

man of wrath and man of mercy
garments stained by anxious blood
man of gold and man of ivory
figure framed by ancient wood

he is the stench of the open grave
he is the stone at the mouth of the cave
he is the lash on the back of the slave
he will not come again

no tyrants cower on their knees
he will not come again
no drunken tears on faces freeze
he will not come again
no hoarded gold in gutters cast
he will not come again
no end to all we know at last
he will not come again

<u>this time it feels right</u>

well, they say:
a whole new day,
will rise and wash
the blackest sins away.
but ours are like a mountain,
and the sunlight
is a wave,
and cycles don't accelerate.
(no matter what they say.)

it's like wine
that's turned to water.
it's like lead
that once was gold.
when she sings the songs
you taught her
don't it make
your blood run cold?

in the hour of abandon,
in the moment of decay,
don't you long to be forgotten
when your love has gone away?

it's like wine

turned into water.
it's like lead
that once was gold.
once she saved you
from the slaughter.
now, your
young love's
growing old.

- - - - -
Some bridges don't burn
they're all concrete and steel
and the more times you cross 'em
the worse that you feel
the more times you cross 'em
the less that you learn
'til one day you realize:
Some bridges don't burn.

Some bridges don't burn
they just keep turnin' up
like a dirty, old coin
in a blind man's cup
and a penny you hate
is a penny you've earned
along with the knowledge:
Some bridges don't burn.
- - - - -

<u>it matters so much</u>

just you and me
through thickness and doubt
dirt sticks to your feet
in a husband house

and prop up the bed
with a stumbling crutch
it matters so much
it matters so much

cigarette flesh
can you save me a fuck
would you do that for me
would you do me that much

with your broken toy truck
and your rag-doll crotch
it matters so much
it matters so much

just me and you
in sickness and parts
the research is finished
and no one got smart

the words come too fast
and the bodies get crushed
it matters so much
it matters so much

just you and me
in erupt and enough
she stitches your cuts
while he buttons your cuffs

like dying inside
but it's only a touch
it matters so much
it matters so much

Jesus Dug A River

Ready every letter for the fire
Steady, ever onward toward the tomb
Careful, every rung of every ladder
Longs to send you spinning to your doom
Capture every father in my kingdom
Drop their bodies deep into the sea
Fasten every manacle of wifedom
Across your heart and body just for me

I am fallen as a child,
Cast down off a mother's knee
Broken, as a five-point star
Become five scattered seeds

Bitter, as a woman
Born to pampered hands and feet
Sickened, by the visage
At the right hand of my seat

Oh, don't you know that Jesus dug a river?
Dug it with a shovel made of bone
For all the tricks inside the bag he carried
The guy could never stand to be alone

Oh, don't you see we muddied up the water?

Dammed it off, and used it as our own
Some day it's gonna flood
From all the teardrops up above
Teardrops falling from a broken throne

- - - - -

Well, there's many a slip
'twixt the cup and the lip.
When I told you I loved you,
I knew that I didn't.
But you'll hear the big click
in just one more minute.
And love it or hate it,
you'll have to forgive it.

I once had a dream
of a sewing machine.
And all that it touched
fell apart at the seams.
But there must be something
more real than it seems.
It must be
in the land
beyond my dreams.

- - - - -

-

The times have changed,
and no one's
leaving babies at your Door.

And no one wants to join
your Ancient Order anymore.

-

A Great and Wasted Friend of Mine

a great and wasted friend of mine
lay down one night to die
he said: you tell me how it ends
I'll meet you by and by

I tried my best to change his mind
but in the end he won
and as he closed his tired eyes
I rose to face the dawn

and it's just enough to break your heart
and keep it broke for good
just enough to let you see
some things that no one should
just enough to let you know
that nothing good lasts long
just some hopeless verses
in a useless little song

a great and wasted friend of mine
came to me in a dream
he said: I hate to let you down
but much is as it seems

few things are more real

than what you put your hands upon
I never missed my fingertips
'til they were fully gone

and it's just enough to make you ache
for someone in your arms
just enough for blood and bone
to sound some deep alarm
just enough to make you wonder
where a dream comes from
just a little splinter
in the center of your palm

Forever Has Only Begun

well, my eyes are sadly shining
like a mirror full of sun
'cause I'm sitting, sadly pining,
for the one who's off and run

here my tears are steady falling
while she laughs behind me eyes
and a bottle's softly calling
and awaiting my reply

and you know that the bottle
can wait forever
that's how long she's gonna be gone
and you know what some folk say
about saying never
forever has only begun

well, my hands are slightly shaking
as the moon it fades from view
and my heart is badly aching
as the dawn comes on anew

somewhere a river's flowing
to a never-ending sea
like the sorrow that is growing

somewhere deep inside of me

and you know that sorrow
can live forever
that's how long she's gonna be gone
yes, every tomorrow's
another forever
forever has only begun

and you know that the devil
can wait forever
forever's how long she'll be gone
and you know what some folk say
about saying never
forever has only begun

- - - - -
i've lost track of the world

i might not have noticed
but morning makes a clerk
of every man

i've lost track of the world

and the notes left behind us
don't add up to whatever
they might have

i've lost track of the world

and i showed so much promise
so many things that
never came to pass

i've lost track of the world

and the world couldn't care less
i can't recall
how anything began
- - - - -

<u>anyone like me</u>

i wish that i recalled
a bit more clearly
what you told me
but it comforted me greatly
at the time

i wish that i had known
the way i now do
that it was you
but you were just so hard
to recognize

and that's the kind of thing
that isn't easy to believe
especially
for anyone like me

no new sun is risen
in this world
or any other
that some darkness has not
driven down before

no desire is awakened
in the heart

of any human
that has not for generations
laid in store

and no man alive
is friendless
at the mercy of another
who will not exchange his burden
for a throne

and though time itself
is endless
and you burn with isolation
you have never for an instant
been alone

but that's the kind of thing
that isn't easy to believe
especially
for anyone like me

i wish i'd never told you
oh, so many things
i told you
i was young and i
was such a fool

and i wish i hadn't listened
then to half
of your responses
but i just thought
you were so fucking cool

and sometimes people need
so much to let themselves believe
especially
anyone like me

<u>the last time I saw you</u>

Years away,
and all between,
still I saw you
        in a dream.
You were leaning
                on a fence that
        I was
        building.

Your eyes were burning wild
    when I turned into a child,
but I think you
        recognized me
            just the same.

Far from the lights of the city.
The last time I saw you alive.
Sunlight was shining so pretty.
Bringing a tear to my eye.

I recall
    a shopping mall
and a movie
            that we saw.
But my eyes

        barely made it
    to the screen.

And the pale light
    of the moon,
    in the early
    days of June,
made your skin shine
                like nothing I'd seen.

Wherever the sunrise might find you,
I hope it gets in your eyes.
I hope they shine like they used to.
I hope you're doing all right.

And I hope the next time I see you,
you're the one dreaming of me.
I hope I shine like I used to.
So bright I'm all that you see.

- - - - -
First: I taught her murder
how I taught it to myself.
First: She was a totem
and she stood for something else.
First: I turned her trigger
'til it pulled all by itself.
First: I sowed disorder
with the seed of broken health.

Next: I took her tongue out
and replaced it with my own.
Next: I propped her guts up
with a jagged, blackened bone.
Next: Her deadened maidenhead
it spit a rabid foam.
Next: I set her spinning,
then I left her all alone.
- - - - -

-

my trials are many
my judges unknown
although they were born
in my skin and my bone

grim specters point fingers
grown thin with decay
from shadows that sunlight
cannot chase away

-

The Devil Ain't Done With Me Yet

Pinch me again
the dream just won't end
There must be something
in the air
The walls slide around
and I'm startled by sounds
and the sex never
goes anywhere

And up with the sun
I'm a party of one
All through the best part
of the day
And wouldn't you know
that it's two for the show
Ain't it funny how
time slips away?

Be patient with me
I'm willing to bet
The Devil Ain't Done
With Me Yet

Don't you cry, darlin'
And, please, don't you fret

The Devil Ain't Done
With Me Yet

You know that I try
It's like blood in my eye
the way that they want
You to slave
I heard the man say
if he had it his way
he'd work you
right into
the grave

And it all makes you feel
like your feelings ain't real
Like not one single
soul understands
And it's all I can do
Not to come home to you
With that horror
all over
my hands

So, hang in there, baby
And take what you get
The Devil Ain't Done
With Me Yet

Like smoke from the fire
Like water is wet
The Devil Ain't Done
With Me Yet

I'll tell you, I know
that we both ought to go
Let's just get the fuck
out of this town
I swear that I heard
in just so many words
there's a whole ton of
shit coming down

And it don't matter where
Honey, I couldn't care
Just as long as you're there
by my side
I'll find us a place
We can both show our face
Like we didn't have
nothing to hide

I'll tell you tomorrow
in case you forget
The Devil Ain't Done

With Me Yet

Hanging Flowers

Who knows what they're climbing from?
Who knows where they're crawling to?
Can you hear that ghostly hum
from their shifting shades of blue?

Hanging flowers
Hanging flowers
Don't they seem to have a way
of closing up around you?

If they sometimes seem quite young
bear in mind they're never new.
You may touch what they've become.
You cannot watch how they grew.

Hanging flowers
Hanging flowers
Don't they seem to have a way
of closing up around you?

posture from heroes
========================

i took what i needed
from here and from there
and i scattered the ashes
all over your chair
i took what i wanted
your means for my ends
my posture from heroes
my weapons from friends

i carried my copies
for months and for years
from city to city
in joy and in tears
i carried my copies
on shoulders bent low
my posture from heroes
my feet in the snow

i dreamt of your words
and i gave up my name
"and now you've decided
to show me the same"
i dreamt of your words
like the thief that i am
my posture from heroes

my head in the sand

i offered you nothing
you needed from me
i balled up tinfoil
and nailed it to trees
i offered you nothing
you snatched it right up
my posture from heroes
my teeth in your cup

-

and though
I've waited longer
than the space
of time
can fill
some small part
inside of me
will wait awhile still

and though the weight
of human lives
are drops
into the sea
there's some small part
enduring
that you'll recognize
in me

-

The Prisoner

Come sit by me stranger, one moment or two
Long dead lies the preacher, confessor make due
What's left of the breath in my chest makes a
terrible sound

My last hours number unspeakably few
My sins are too many to bear witness to
My body is broken, my spirit sleeps under the
ground

My story is written in Sorrow's dark pen
The stench of my life is the sweat of caged men
I've payed all my days with my flesh, measured
penny for pound

I dreamt once of greatness, as does every man
And felt that dream crumble to dust in my hands
And, hopeless, surrendered that dust to the
scalding wind

I spoke once a language of rain and of sand
A language my tongue will no longer command
The words I speak now are grotesque as a
corpses' grin

All angels must fall from the head of the pin
The noblest intentions make monsters of men
The blood of the saints is as black as a river
of sin

The arms I extended in love and in trust
Came back to me covered in blood and in rust
And in this foul prison I've answered for all
that I've done

So here at the end of a road made of bone
I lie in the arms of a god made of stone
What frightens me most is the thought that it's
only begun

Through judgement I've lived and to judgement I
die
Somewhere in the distance; an infants cry
All night becomes day in the face of a terrible
sun

<u>heart full of spleen</u>

no, my right hand don't know
where my left wants to go
there are many things i've never seen
but some things i have heard
in his long-buried words
i have heard with a heart full of spleen

if you can't hate like me
you won't ever be free
to see how the fire burns clean
and you never will know
what the rest of us know
know the world with a heart full of spleen

all my scared boys and girls
who have built their own worlds
'cause they couldn't quite find the right scene
in their dreams have been told
they won't ever grow old
by the voice of a heart full of spleen

it was torn from my chest
when i paused just to rest
and replaced with some awful machine
it's grown thin as a Host

but i carry it close
carry on with a heart full of spleen

so my blood may not run
like once when i was young
and the poor thing might look quite obscene
but it beats on and on
and my foot taps along
to the sound of my heart full of spleen

i have dreamt of your face
like some porcelain vase
that i smash just to liven up things
and i smile all night
'til the first rising light
hits the top of my heart full of spleen

-

and with just a little practice
soon I learned I could control it

and with just a little practice
soon I learned I could control it

and with just a little practice
soon I learned I could control it
-

Thaddeus Denton lives and writes outside of
Providence, RI.

www.ingramcontent.com/pod-product-compliance
Lightning Source LLC
Chambersburg PA
CBHW031326040426
42443CB00005B/227